THE
LANGUAGE
PARTS
CATALOG

The World's Finest Selection of
NEW AND IMPROVED PARTS FOR YOUR BRAIN,
Guaranteed to Make Sounds, Words, Sentences,
and Large Language Chunks
Work Better for You

Catalog compiled by
Dr. Mel Levine

Educators Publishing Service, Inc.
Cambridge and Toronto

DEDICATION

The Language Parts Catalog is dedicated to the enduring memory of Kay Hains, who worked for many years at the Clinical Center for the Study of Development and Learning as a tireless believer in children. Kay made use of her extraordinary kind of mind to advocate for the well-being of struggling kids, their parents, and their teachers. Among other talents, she had superb language skills with which to communicate and act on her commitment. Thanks, Kay. You will always be remembered and profoundly missed.

SOME THANKFUL LANGUAGE

Dr. Mel Levine, the author of *The Language Parts Catalog,* would like to thank a number of people who helped create it. The catalog benefited from the great artwork and imagination of Joshua Taylor, a teacher of very young children. When he was a student, Joshua liked school because it was a place where he could draw lots of pictures (often when he should have been listening to his teacher). Jen Noon edited the catalog and had to work hard and with amazing skill to correct all of Dr. Levine's mistakes (and improve his language). Dr. Levine is co-chairman of the board of All Kinds of Minds, an organization designed to help students understand differences in learning and use their minds well. He is grateful to all the board members, who have supported and encouraged his work. Dr. Levine is also the director of the Clinical Center for the Study of Development and Learning, and he wants to thank the Administration on Developmental Disabilities and the Bureau of Maternal and Child Health (both in Washington, D.C.) for their support of the Center. Finally, he wants to thank all the talkative animals on Sanctuary Farm (where he and his wife live) for all their love and for what they have taught him about their particular language parts!

Educators Publishing Service, Inc.

Design by Joyce C. Weston

ISBN 0-8388-1980-x
Printed in U.S.A.

CONTENTS

INTRODUCTION

Humor is a cool way to learn. It is great to be able to find out about something complicated and important and have a few laughs at the same time. This catalog is not real; it's meant to make fun of some of the catalogs most people get all the time in the mail. But the subject is no laughing matter. *The Language Parts Catalog* is all about one of the human brain's most important jobs. The ability to understand and use language affects almost everything you do in life.

Language is crucial. Some people have really good language skills, while others have big weaknesses in their language ability. Kids who have language problems can have a very difficult time in school and in other aspects of their lives. Unfortunately, too many students are struggling with language problems without even knowing that they have these weaknesses. They may think that they're dumb or just not too bright, but that's not true. They are smart in ways that don't involve a lot of language. *The Language Parts Catalog* can help these kids find out about the specific language weaknesses that could be interfering with their learning and even preventing them from enjoying school.

Very few students completely understand what language is and what it does. That's partly because language is so complicated. Language ability is made up of many different parts. It's possible for a person to have some language parts that work really well and other parts that are a problem. It is very sad when a kid has a problem with one or more language parts and doesn't even know it. It could be that his or her parents and teacher don't even realize what the problem is. Then no one can work on improving or fixing it.

The Language Parts Catalog can teach you about all the most important parts of language. It can also help you think about your own language ability, including which parts you think are strong and which ones might be weak, or maybe even getting in the way of your learning. *The Language Parts Catalog* encourages you to make believe that you can order spare parts for your brain to improve your language ability. You order whatever new parts you think you need, using the order form near the end of the catalog. In completing this form, you are actually rating your own language strengths and weaknesses. Knowing where you're strong and where you can improve can help you and others to understand your kind of mind. Of course, new parts for your brain are not really available (at least not yet!). Also, remember that you are using your imagination while reading through this catalog, so the parts listed are not actually the names of parts of your brain. They are functions or jobs your mind does. In many cases, scientists and doctors don't even know exactly the spot in your brain where language missions (like knowing the sound a letter makes) are accomplished.

The Language Parts Catalog is meant to be an entertaining way to learn all about the parts of language. Understanding these language parts and what they do can definitely help you improve your language abilities. As you read on, you will discover that the language parts fit into six different language systems, listed below:

- The Language Sound Processing System
- The Word Meaning System
- The Sentence Sense Maker System
- The Discourse Developer System

THE LANGUAGE SYSTEMS AND THEIR PARTS

1. The Language Sound Processing System
The Rapid Sound Sensor
The Language Sound Transmitter
The Rhymer
The Sound-to-Symbol Attacher
The Sound Splitter
The Sound Blender
The Foreign Sound Processor
The Sound Inflector
The Language Sound Finder
The Total Language Sound Processor

2. The Word Meaning System
The Word Builder
The Semantic Network Builder
The Vocabulary Memorizer
The Word Meaning Stretcher
The Technical Word Learner
The Abstract Word Learner
The Written Word Decoder
The Word Classifier

3. The Sentence Sense Maker System
The Grammar Applicator and Checker
The Sentence Writer
The Speedy Sentence Synthesizer
The Speedy Sentence Translator

The Sentence Reader
The Figurative Figure-er
The Conjunctionizer

4. The Discourse Developer System
The Reading and Listening Recorder
The Sentence Meaning Combiner
The Discourse Sequencer
The Paraphraser-Summarizer
The Written Language Blender

5. The Language Transmission System
The Thought Arranger
The Speech Clarifier
The Fluency Lubricator
The Stall Uninstaller
The Language Elaborator
The Creative Thought Generator
The Missing Word and Name Locator

6. The Language Socializer System
The Code Switcher
The Mood Processor
The Mood Matcher
The Topic Selector and Timer
The Humor Regulator
The Conflict Solver
The Language Lingo Learner
The Social Language Interpreter

- The Language Transmission System
- The Language Socializer System

Together these language systems make up your mind's overall language ability. In this catalog, each system and its parts are described in a different section. You will soon find out that the human mind has many different language parts. These are listed in the table you see above. Don't try to learn them all now. This table just gives you an overall picture of the different language parts that will be discussed in this catalog.

Instead of actually receiving new brain parts in the mail, you might need to get help with the parts of your language ability that need some fixing up. A language specialist, a teacher or tutor, and even you (yes, you) can work to improve specific parts of your language ability. Improving can take a lot of practice, effort, and time, but it sure is worth it. You'll appreciate all the incredible things that good language skills can do as you read through *The Language Parts Catalog*.

The following list of questions can help you begin to decide if you *might* be having problems with language demands in school and elsewhere.

QUESTIONS TO THINK ABOUT

Yes No

❑ ❑ Does schoolwork get to be too much work for you?

❑ ❑ Do you sometimes have trouble understanding your teachers?

❑ ❑ Does your mind "tune out" in classes where there's a lot of language?

❑ ❑ Do you find yourself looking around in class to see what others are doing when the teacher gives instructions?

❑ ❑ Was it hard for you to learn to read well?

❑ ❑ Do you read too slowly?

❑ ❑ Do you have trouble understanding what you read?

❑ ❑ Are word problems the hardest part of math for you?

❑ ❑ Do you dislike writing?

❑ ❑ Do you have good ideas that you can't write down well?

❑ ❑ Are you a person who has good ideas but has trouble putting your thinking into words?

❑ ❑ Do you get confused about grammar and punctuation?

❑ ❑ Is it hard for you to spell accurately?

❑ ❑ Do you hate to be called on in class?

❑ ❑ Do you keep using words like *stuff* and *like* and *uhh* because you have trouble remembering more exact words?

❑ ❑ Are you afraid to call people on the telephone because you may not know what to say?

❑ ❑ Do you have trouble sounding "cool" when you want to?

❑ ❑ Do people think you sound angry when you don't feel angry?

If the answer to three or more of these questions is "yes," then you may need to order one or more of our language parts for your mind. If you just have one or two of these problems, you may or may not want to fix them up. So read this catalog carefully and fill out the attached order form. As you will discover, there are many different parts of language, and we offer new parts for any of your language needs.

As you read through the catalog, think about these questions and about the descriptions of the language parts. On some pages, you'll find a space to take notes (if you want to) about which parts you think you might need.

Dear <u>Language Parts Catalog</u> People,

I have always been a person with good ideas and a whole lot of knowledge. But, sadly, other people just didn't realize how intelligent I was. That was because it was so hard for me to say my ideas in a way others could understand easily. I used to get frustrated in class when I had such important things to say, but it took me too long to figure out how to say them. I would get totally uptight as I sat in the classroom. I was in constant fear that the teacher would call on me and I would make a fool of myself when I tried to answer, even though I knew the answer. Then one day my best friend felt sorry for me and gave me a copy of your catalog. He didn't say much, but he opened it to the section about language transmission. I couldn't believe my eyes. Those language parts were just the ones I needed. I ordered them and started working on my Language Transmission System. Now I can find words, speak in complete sentences, and communicate my complicated ideas. I can even do this when I write. It took a lot of practice and some risk taking. Now I am running for class president and making a whole lot of speeches. I can't believe it's me. Thank you, <u>Language Parts Catalog</u>. I would like you to send me more copies to give to other kids in school. After reading the catalog I realized how many other students are struggling with language, and they don't even realize it.

Your Friend and Future President,

Agnes

Agnes
One W
Lincoln

What Is Language, Anyway?

We use the word *language* all the time in school, but believe it or not, it's hard to understand what language really is. This is partly because we use language to talk about or even think about language. Also, language has many parts to it and it gets used in hundreds of different ways in school and out of school. What do *you* think language is?

_____

_____

_____

Here are some of the characteristics of language:

✓ **Language is a code, almost like a secret code.** It's a way of translating ideas that are in someone's mind into sounds and symbols that someone else can figure out. Imagine making up your own language; it might sound great, but no one else would understand your code.

✓ **Language helps you think.** Words and sentences can be the tools you use to build your understanding of something, to create your own ideas, and to solve problems. Try to practice thinking about something first without language and then with language.

✓ **Language helps you remember.** It is often a lot easier to remember something later if you put it into words first.

✓ **Language is social.** It helps you share your interests with other kids. If you don't use the same kind of language as other kids, it may be harder to make and keep friends.

✓ **Language has a bunch of sounds in it.** They are called **phonemes**. In English there are about 44 sounds, yet there are only 26 letters. So, some sounds must have more than one letter in them, and some letters must have more than one sound. Can you think of some sounds that contain two or more letters? One example is the word *play*, where the *a* and the *y* make one sound. Notice that language sounds don't mean anything. If someone walked around just saying, "Th!", no one would know what she was talking about. They might even think she was a little weird, even though she'd be using a very good language sound.

✓ **Language sounds are put together to form words.** Unlike phonemes (language sounds), words have meanings. A lot of words, in fact, have many meanings that depend upon the sentences they're in. Using real language sounds, can you make up some words that have *no* meaning? You may want to keep these in your desk, just in case someday you come across a meaning that needs a word!

✓ **Words get put together to make sentences.** Sentences have to follow rules. That is, the words have to be in the right order or people will say, "Sorry, that's not good English." The rules are called **grammatical rules.** Sometimes these rules are hard or don't seem to make sense, but you're supposed to follow them anyway. Otherwise, people will have trouble understanding you, and what's the point of using language if you're not understood? The order of words strongly affects the meaning of a sentence. "Suzanne chased the dog" obviously means something different from "The dog chased Suzanne," even though both sentences contain the same language sounds and words. Sentences are meant to be meaningful; they are supposed to make sense in addition to using good word order. Think about the difference between saying "Ben climbed the tree" and "The tree climbed Ben."

✓ **Language also comes in large servings.** Big chunks of language have lots of sentences in them and are called **discourse.**

Discourse is a whole story or set of directions or explanations. When you're reading whole paragraphs, passages, chapters, or an entire book, you are reading discourse. Because it is long, discourse takes up a lot of space in a part of your memory called **active working memory**. This is where your brain stores what was contained on one part of a page while you're reading the rest of the page. It would be a shame if you forgot the first part of a story while reading its ending. You need to remember the whole thing. Can you think of times when you've been able to understand and laugh at a joke but then couldn't remember it to tell your friend?

✓ **Your language abilities can help you to learn another language.** Once your mind is good with the language your family uses, it can go on and add another language (like Russian if it's not your first language). There are also some kids who grow up speaking two or more different languages. This is common in families that move from one country to another, or when the parents are from different countries. Some people find that learning and speaking a second language actually makes the first one work especially well.

✓ **Language helps you appreciate a lot of things.** If you know the name for something, it is sometimes easier to enjoy it. For example, if you know a particular dog is called a schnauzer, you might find it more interesting than if you just called it a dog. People who know the names of different makes of cars or different birds actually notice their details better. While trying to attach a name to something, they are likely to look more closely at the thing they are trying to identify. You don't have to examine something too well to say it's a bird, but you have to look much more closely to call it a robin.

✓ **Language is good for entertainment.** Jokes, song lyrics, and the words in movies and TV shows are all forms of language fun. Some people have a good time talking on the telephone.

✓ **Language comes in many forms.** In addition to spoken and written language, there are sign language and body language. Do you know what they are and how they are used?

✓ **There are parts of the human brain that specialize in language.** They are called **language centers** and can be seen in Figure 1. These brain areas figure out what people are saying to you, and they enable you to put your ideas into language.

As you may have noticed by now, using and understanding language is absolutely crucial for success in school. In fact, it can be more

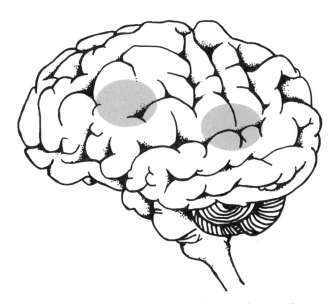

Figure 1. This is a side view of the human brain. The two main language centers are on the left side, as shown by the shaded areas above.

important in school than it is when you grow up. When you get to be an adult, you can choose a job that has lots of language in it or one that has much less language (every job has some). School always has huge amounts of language. Most learning and a large part of the schoolwork you have to do uses the language code. So if you're not too good with language, it is likely that school will be hard for you and not much fun.

Different kids show different language abilities. Some students are great with language, while others are very smart but not so good with language. Instead, they may have other good qualities, such as great spatial abilities. That means they are excellent at picturing things in their mind, understanding how things work, and being able to design or build something. But their minds don't work as smoothly with one or more of the parts of language. These students may be said to have **language dysfunction**. There are many forms of this weakness. Some kids mostly have trouble with the language sounds, others with learning word meanings, and still others with the big chunks of language (discourse). Some students are better at understanding language than they are at getting their ideas into language. Others are just the opposite: they talk or even write better than they understand. In fact, everybody has strengths and weaknesses in different parts of language. That's why we have this catalog—so you can find out what you need in order to be better with language.

SECTION 1

The Language Sound
Processing System

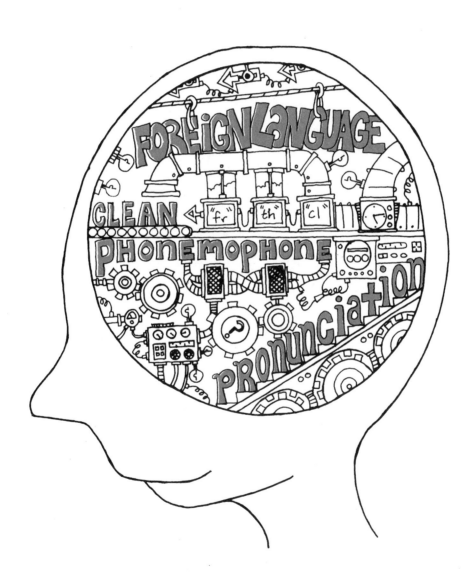

THE LANGUAGE SOUND PROCESSING SYSTEM

Designed especially for use during school, the Language Sound Processing System helps students' minds sort out the sounds inside words. Equipped with an excellent Language Sound Processing System, your mind can easily break down a word into its sounds. These sounds are called **phonemes** (different from phonies or ponies). Your ability to process them is your **phonological awareness.** Most people can recognize immediately that the word *cap* is made of three sounds: k-a-p. Our minds need to be able to do this well, especially when we're first learning to read. Kids who can't figure out and split up the language sounds (the phonemes) in words can have a hard time learning to read easily and fast enough.

Remember that almost everyone is born with a Language Sound Processing System in her or his brain. But how well does it work? Are you satisfied with yours?

Here are some of the truly amazing jobs your Language Sound Processing System can do when it's working well. Read this list and begin to think about whether you need to fix up some parts in your current Language Sound Processing System.

✓ It can help you tell the difference between words that sound a lot alike, such as *bowl* and *ball*. Can you think of some other pairs of confusing words it could help with?

✓ It can help you spell. If your mind has a good sense of language sounds, then there are many words you won't misspell. For example, you'll know how to spell the word *path* because your Language Sound Processing System will know what letters make up the sounds in the word.

✓ It can help you match language sounds with groups of letters, so you get to know which language sounds go together with *fr, th, cl,* and other combinations. The Language Sound Processing System helps you file those letters with their sounds in your memory. That way you can recognize them when you read and recall them when you need to spell.

✓ It can help you rhyme words, so you can write a rhyming poem or cool lyrics to a song.

✓ It can help you pronounce words more accurately and easily.

✓ It makes it easier to understand what people are telling you. Of course, there are many other parts of your mind needed to understand language. (Check out the other sections of this catalog; they are all crucial.)

✓ It can help you learn another language. If your mind is very good with the sounds in your own language, it makes it much easier to learn a foreign language. A lot of English-speaking kids who have trouble learning French or Spanish or some other language may be only poor to fair when it comes to processing English language sounds. Some people who come to the United States from other countries have trouble learning English because the Language Sound Processing System for their own language doesn't work so well.

How about you, how well do you think your Language Sound Processing System works? Now read the descriptions of replacement parts for this system, and think about what you might need and how badly you might need it. After you have read the explanations of each part, please use the enclosed order form to record what you think you need and how much you think you could use it.

Language Sound Processing Parts

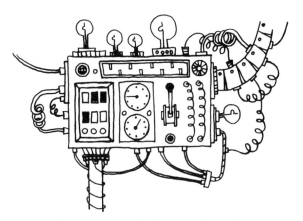

THE RAPID SOUND SENSOR

This astonishing language part allows you to process word sounds at lightning speed. Did you know that in school there is nothing your brain has to do faster than figure out language sounds? A language sound may only last 40 milliseconds (and then it's gone). That means 25 of them can fit into just one second! If your mind cannot interpret language sounds fast enough, there's a good chance you'll have trouble in school. With a Rapid Sound Sensor that works well, you can read fast, spell fast, and understand people when they talk fast. That's because all words are made out of language sounds, whether you read them, hear them, or put them on paper. The sounds in words provide loads of information about their meanings and spellings. If fast language sounds seem to you like a big blur, consider ordering the Rapid Sound Sensor.

THE LANGUAGE SOUND TRANSMITTER

This part helps you pronounce language sounds quickly and distinctly, so it is easy for others to understand what you are trying to say. It works closely with the Language Transmission System (see page 39) when you need to say or write something. It can be fun to use this part to copy the way other people speak. Do you find yourself slurring or running your words together when you talk? Do your listeners always say "What?" Then order this part!

THE RHYMER

This entertaining part makes it easier for you to recognize when two or more words have the same sounds in them—mainly at their endings. That way you can tell when words rhyme. Do song lyrics and poetry sound dull to you? Maybe they have rhymes you're missing out on. With this part, you can even write your own rhymes!

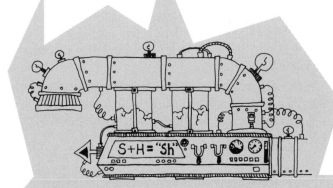

THE SOUND-TO-SYMBOL ATTACHER

This valuable part helps you attach specific language sounds to groups of letters (like $s + h$ = the sound sh) and then file them in your memory for future use. This part is absolutely critical for learning to read and spell. You may want to get it if you have trouble remembering what groups of letters sound like.

NOTES

_____

_____

_____

_____

THE SOUND SPLITTER

This crucial part helps you to sound out a word you haven't seen or maybe even heard before. If you can't pronounce individual sounds to put together a whole word, you will want to order the Sound Splitter.

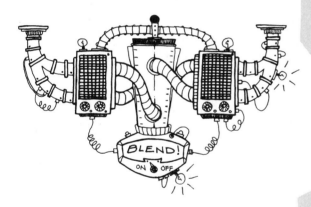

THE SOUND BLENDER

This important part lets you put together sounds to build a word while speaking. It is also very helpful for reading and spelling. Without it, you may have trouble forming or recognizing words. If you have this problem, you should get yourself a Sound Blender.

THE FOREIGN SOUND PROCESSOR

This new imported part fits in the sound system needed to learn a foreign language. It comes in a version for every language in the world. But remember, it needs to be plugged into your first Language Sound Processing System. If your first system isn't working very well, we can't guarantee that the foreign language system will operate. If learning a new language is giving you trouble, give this part a try.

THE SOUND INFLECTOR

This inexpensive part helps you put the correct emphasis on certain sounds or syllables within a word. If you know the word but can't say it quite right, the Sound Inflector may help.

THE LANGUAGE SOUND FINDER

This is a convenient part, one that helps you to use language sounds to strengthen the way your memory works. That way you can recall things by how they sound. You might say to yourself, "I can't quite remember that kid's name, but I know it begins with 'Day'. . . . Oh, yes, now I remember—his name is David." Does this memory trick sound new to you? Then you might need the Language Sound Finder.

If you think you need all of these Language Sound Processing System parts, consider ordering our Total Language Sound Processor, a completely installed unit that combines all of the above parts into a very sound sound operation.

Dear <u>Language Parts Catalog</u> People:

I am so thrilled with my improved Language Sound Processing System. I don't know how to thank you.

When I was first starting out in school, I had a very hard time learning to read. Then I had big-time problems with spelling, too. Other kids were becoming great readers and spellers, and I could hardly read or write. I got plenty of extra help, but I could never remember which sounds went with which letters. I felt completely stupid. Then I got your excellent catalog and realized that I was an intelligent kid who had a small problem with my language sound system. My mind just wasn't good at processing those phonemes (or are they phomenes?). It was almost impossible for me to know how certain language sounds were put together to form whole words. Once I understood my problem clearly, I could work on it and practice with language sounds. Of course, I also bought some of your truly amazing Language Sound Processor System parts and kept working on my language.

Thank you, <u>Language Parts Catalog</u>. I have given a copy to my little sister, who is having trouble learning to read. I guess it runs in our family.

Your Friend,
Sonny

Sonny C
35 Holly
Los Palos,

✂ AN IMPORTANT REMINDER!
Language sounds have no meanings. They are just plain sounds. If you would like to add real meaning to language (not a bad idea), then read on in this catalog, and learn about the oportunities that await the proud owners of an excellent Word Meaning System.

SECTION 2
The Word Meaning System

THE WORD MEANING SYSTEM

How good is your mind at understanding and using words really well? Knowing a lot of words is important. Knowing a lot about the words you know is even more important! Your mind is like a huge dictionary. By the time you're five years old, your brain contains about 10,000 words. After that you learn thousands more each year. But there's a lot of variation. Some people have minds that are like word magnets, so new words just stick to them every day. Other people just want to keep using and under-standing only words they already know.

The meanings of words are filed away in your mind in what is called your **semantic network**. (*Semantics* means words and their meanings. The semantic network is your Word Meaning System.) A semantic network is like a dictionary full of words that are all connected to each other in some way. It is the collection of words and their meanings that you have stored in your memory so you can find them when you need them. When it's working well, your semantic network can do the following things:

✓It can help you understand what people are saying, especially when they use big or uncommon words.

✓It can help you learn and understand more words so you can talk and write about more ideas.

✓It can help you express your own ideas more easily to make you sound more intelligent.

✓It can add room in your memory; it's easier to remember something when you put it in words and even whisper it under your breath. If you need to remember which socket wrench you need to fix your bike, it is easier to remember if you say to yourself, "It's the medium-sized socket wrench" instead of just picturing the tool in your mind. Of course, that means you need to have the word for *wrench* and the words for *socket wrench* stored somewhere in your semantic network.

✓It can help you learn a new language. The more easily you learn words in your first lan-guage, the easier it is to add words to a new foreign language semantic network.

✓It can help you learn about complicated subjects. Many school subjects are full of new words. They may be words you don't use very often. Usually, to learn a new subject (like biology or the history of a coun-try or even mathematics), you have to master a long list of pretty tough new words. You need to understand these words and be able to use them very soon after you meet them for the first time—that's not so easy. It can actually be a challenge to put new words in your semantic network and then find them and use them when you need to.

Word Meaning Parts

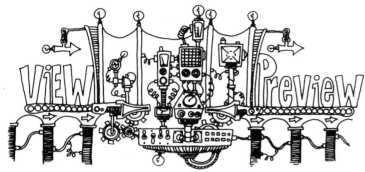

aware of the parts of words, you will read, spell, and learn the meanings of new words much more easily. How good is your parts of words part? If you're having a tough time creating whole words from word parts, give this part a try.

THE WORD BUILDER

This is a great part that makes it quite easy to build whole words out of parts of words. The parts are called **morphemes**. They include groups of letters like *ing, ed, ly,* and *ism.* Morphemes are like bricks. In a building, the same kind of brick could be used in many different ways. In the same way, morphemes like *ing* can be used in many different ways to build words. For example, the morpheme *pre* means "before." If you put it with *view*, it becomes *preview*, and with *pare*, it becomes *prepare*. If you are

THE SEMANTIC NETWORK BUILDER

This part takes words you know and puts them on an imaginary map with other words. The semantic network in your mind contains words that are similar or opposite in meaning or that are related to each other in any way. People who are great with words are able to see the similarities and differences between thousands of words. They can use this part to develop a fantastic semantic network, so those thousands of words in their minds can connect to each other in thousands of ways. An example of part of a semantic network can be seen in Figure 2. Imagine your mind containing millions of

A Section of a Semantic Network

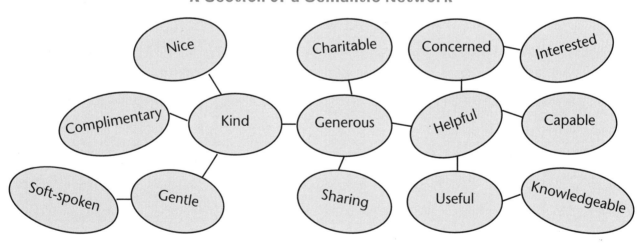

Figure 2. This diagram shows how words are supposed to get stored in your mind as part of a huge semantic network. Within the network, words are filed next to other words that have meaningful connections with them. This makes it easier to find a different word when the one you're about to use doesn't quite say what you want it to say.

word connections. As you get older, your network connects more and more words. As you go through school, your semantic network can become more densely populated with words, which connect with similar or even opposite words in the network. That way you can file, find, and understand words much more easily. Do you have a good enough semantic network? Or are you one of those kids whose mind contains too many unconnected words—words that don't ever make you think of other words? If the words in your memory don't connect to each other enough, become the proud owner of a new and improved semantic network by ordering this part. Your grades in school and your understanding of language will improve unbelievably when you plug in the Semantic Network Builder and start using it.

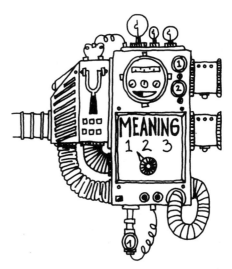

THE WORD MEANING STRETCHER

Words can have many different meanings depending on how they're used. You can say, "Put this soup back on the stove; it's much too *cool*." Or you can say, "Joe's a great guy; he's really *cool*." Or you can say, "Mira, you're talking too much. *Cool* it, please." Students who are excellent with word meanings know a lot about the different meanings that words have. Each part of this catalog talks about a different language part, but even the word *part* has a lot of possible meanings. Two of those meanings are "leave a place" or "a line that separates one section of your hair from another section." There are also words that include the word *part*, including *partly*, *partition*, and *partake*. Remember, it isn't how many words you know that counts; it's how well you understand the different meanings of the words you know. That's why words need to be stretched out in your mind to cover all their possible meanings. Can you do this? If not, consider ordering this part.

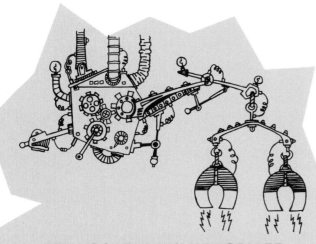

THE VOCABULARY MEMORIZER

This valuable part is just what you need if you have trouble learning new vocabulary words in school. The Vocabulary Memorizer helps you store words so you can understand, recall, and use them in the future. Some kids have a very hard time learning new words, but with the Vocabulary Memorizer, new words stick in your mind like glue (at least until you take the test in school the next day).

NOTES

_____

_____

_____

THE TECHNICAL WORD LEARNER

This part helps you learn and remember the meanings of words that you discover in school and use almost entirely in school. All the tough words you meet in science and mathematics are included. Words like *hypotenuse, photosynthesis, rhombus,* and *molecule* can be easy to misunderstand and even easier to forget! These are technical words, words that you and your friends don't use every day. Your best friend doesn't ask you how your molecules are doing! With the Technical Word Learner, you will awe everyone with your complete command of these difficult words. If technical words make your head spin, you'll want to try this part.

THE ABSTRACT WORD LEARNER

Abstract words are words that describe or name things that are hard to picture in your mind. As you go on with your education in school, you meet more and more new abstract words that you absolutely must understand well. The Abstract Word Learner helps your mind translate abstract words into their meanings. Words like *sportsmanship, sympathy, democracy,* and *creative* are abstract. Concrete words are the opposite of abstract words and include *hammer, music, sneakers, crispy, jumping, round,* and *smoothly.* Concrete words describe something that you understand by using your senses—something you can see, touch, taste, smell, or hear. Some kids are only good with concrete words; they can't stand all the abstract words they have to learn and use all the time in school. If this describes you, don't miss out or mess up. Go for it—order the Abstract Word Learner.

THE WRITTEN WORD DECODER

Words on a page are like some kind of secret code that your mind has to translate into word sounds and meanings. This crucial part allows you to look at a written word (such as in a book or on a street sign) and know its meaning and sounds instantly, even without having to pronounce the word in your mind or say it out loud. This part is obviously very important if you are to become a fast and accurate reader. Are written words still an unbroken code for you? Do you need to say them or think about them to figure out their meaning and sounds? If so, you need the Written Word Decoder.

THE WORD CLASSIFIER

This phenomenal part makes it possible for you to completely understand parts of speech and how they are supposed to work. With this part, you can know exactly which words are nouns, which are verbs, which are adjectives, and which are adverbs. As a result, you will not use these words the wrong way, and you will understand other people better when they are using parts of speech. If parts of speech confuse you, or you have trouble remembering which ones are which, consider ordering the Word Classifier.

Dear Language Parts People:

I am a person of few words. Words have never been my strong point. I am great at sports, fantastic in math, and truly talented in art class. But, sadly, I have never been great with words. I get stumped all the time when I read or hear a hard word. Others seem to figure it out, but that's incredibly hard for me. Also, I hate it when we have to memorize vocabulary words. It is so boring, and I can't remember the words anyway. I like to keep using the same words over and over again.

Recently a friend of mine lent me your fantastic catalog. I recognized myself in the section on the Word Meaning System. I realized that in the next few years, school is going to explode with new vocabulary, so I can't keep using those same words all the time. I just can't wait to get my new language parts, so I can build a better semantic network. I am already working on it. Please rush my order.

Yours in a Hurry to Succeed,
Tony

Tony B
167 Nu
Concor

SECTION 3
The Sentence
Sense Maker System

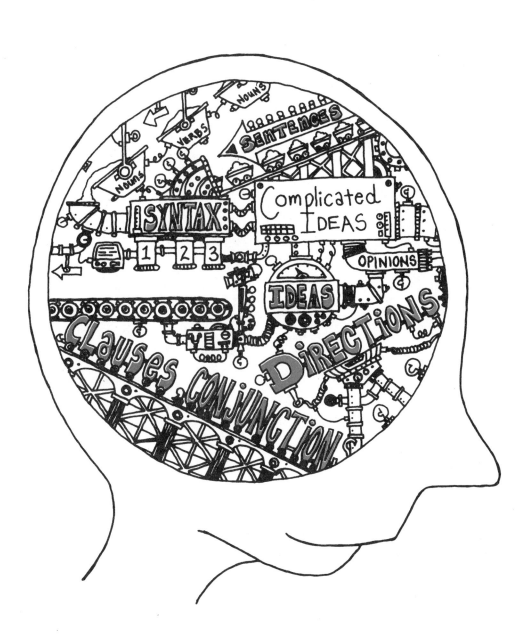

THE SENTENCE SENSE MAKER SYSTEM

As we all know, words are put together to construct sentences. Sentences are more than just phrases. "As good as it gets" is a phrase, while "This raspberry ice cream is as good as it gets" is a complete sentence. Unlike phrases or a few words you mumble, sentences are forced to follow strict rules. They have to contain certain parts of speech (such as nouns and verbs). Also, sentences have to mean something, and the order of words in a sentence has a lot to do with what it will mean. The order of words within a sentence is called *syntax* (pronounced SIN-tacks).

Everyone's brain contains a Sentence Sense Maker System, which has many important jobs to perform. Some of these jobs are listed below:

✓It helps you express complicated ideas, with the help of your Language Transmission System (see page 39).

✓It helps you understand other people's complicated ideas.

✓It helps you give and receive directions, such as how to find the video store or do a certain type of math problem.

✓It helps you figure out complex sentences, which are sentences with clauses and conjunctions (words such as *and, or, because, until, unless,* and *although*).

✓It can help you clarify and understand your own ideas and opinions by putting your thoughts into sentences. There's an old saying that goes, "How can I know what I think until I hear what I say?"

✓It helps you understand sentences that have more than one meaning. You can see some examples in the table below.

SENTENCE MEANINGS

Sentence	One Meaning	Another Meaning
She keeps on beating him.	She often hits him.	She wins a lot of games.
That dog seems to enjoy smelling.	He likes having a bad odor.	He often sniffs things.
I'm tied up right now.	I am very busy.	I can't move until someone takes these ropes off me!
Alan is that very big rock collector.	He is a large person who collects rocks.	He collects large rocks. Or: He is a famous rock collector.
Elisa wanted to come in first.	She preferred to come inside before she did anything else.	She hoped to win the race.
Steve was glad he saw the bus stop.	He was pleased that he got to see where to catch the bus.	He was pleased to see the bus come to a halt.

Sentence Sense Maker Parts

THE GRAMMAR APPLICATOR AND CHECKER

This unique part helps you make use of grammar rules to build sentences that are in excellent English. It also assists you in listening to or reading sentences and deciding if their grammar is decent. The Checker part of this part helps you edit and proofread sentences to make sure they're correct. If your homework comes back with lots of corrections to your sentences, or you have trouble checking your work for correctness, then this is the part for you.

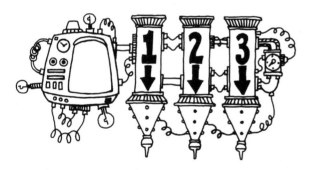

THE SENTENCE WRITER

This popular part lets you combine your knowledge of words with your knowledge of sentence building to write great sentences. It will help you produce good reports and score well on essay tests in school. Is writing sentences taking too much time and effort? To get excellent with writing, order this part.

THE SPEEDY SENTENCE SYNTHESIZER

Excellent sentences often have to be built fast. This efficient part helps you build correct sentences really quickly, so that your language can capture your ideas as fast as they are produced by your mind. Don't be caught with ideas that you can't get into words and sentences. If your ideas are trapped inside your head, set them free! Order this part and get speedy.

THE SPEEDY SENTENCE TRANSLATOR

This complex part helps you understand other people's sentences when they talk; it, too, has to operate at tremendous speed, since most people speak very fast. If you get left behind in school because teachers seem to talk too fast, if you find yourself looking around to see what others are doing because you can't keep up with the flow of language instructions, then you can't afford to wait much longer. Treat yourself to the Speedy Sentence Translator.

THE SENTENCE READER

Reading is very dependent upon good language skills. This miraculous part lets you read and understand sentences by figuring out both the meanings of the words and the ways in which the word order and grammar of a sentence affect its meaning. If reading and understanding sentences is a big struggle, give the Sentence Reader a try.

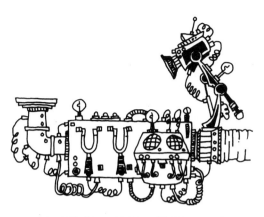

THE FIGURATIVE FIGURE-ER

There are many expressions that don't really mean what they seem to mean when you define the words. For example, if you ask some people, "Can I give you a hand?", you're not offering to take your hand off and give it to them. You just want to help them out. This kind of expression is known as a **figure of speech.** Language that uses figures of speech is called **figurative language.** Language that means exactly what the words mean is called **literal language.** If you say, "It's literally raining cats and dogs," that means that cats and dogs are really falling out of the sky. The table below shows you some more examples of figurative expressions and their literal meanings.

Can you think of any figurative sentences? They're fun to create.

There are many kids who have problems interpreting figurative language, and there is a lot of figurative language in everyday life. If you are too concrete (that means you take language too literally), then you should

FIGURATIVE VS. LITERAL

Sentence	Figurative Meaning	Literal Meaning
You'd better hit the road.	You need to leave now.	You should slap the street or bang it with a hammer.
You should go out on a limb.	Take a chance.	Climb a tree.
You're all wet.	You are wrong about something.	You need to dry off with a towel.
You have your hands full.	You are busy.	You are holding things in both hands.
You're at the end of your rope.	You've tried everything and are discouraged.	You need to get some more rope.
Cool it!	Relax!	Put it in the refrigerator.
She's in hot water.	The girl is in trouble.	She could burn herself in the bathtub.
That book is way over his head.	The book is too hard for him.	The book is on a very high shelf.
Jeff has an open mind.	Jeff is willing to consider new ideas.	Jeff has a hole in his head!
It's time to turn over a new leaf.	You need to be different from now on.	Find a recently fallen leaf on the ground and flip it over.

consider ordering our fine Figurative Figure-er. That way you can understand the message people are really trying to give you. This part can also help you speak in figurative language; if you understand these figures of speech, you can use them yourself and make your speech more colorful and fun.

THE CONJUNCTIONIZER

This fabulous part lets you use and understand the words that attach clauses (parts of sentences) to the middles or the ends of sentences. This language part helps you use such words as *and, or, but, unless, although,* and even everyone's favorite, *notwithstanding* (whatever that means). If you want to be able to use sentences like "I'll meet you at the park, unless it's raining," be sure to order the Conjunctionizer.

A LETTER FROM AN UNDERSTANDING CUSTOMER

Dear <u>Language Parts Catalog</u> Publisher:

I used to get so confused in class. When a teacher gave directions there were times when I had to look around to see what everyone else was doing. I started to tune out a lot because I didn't understand what was going on. Everyone thought I was having trouble with my attention. But really I stopped listening because I couldn't keep up with all the complicated sentences my teacher used. I was also having major grief with reading comprehension. My writing was a problem because I only liked to use short and simple sentences, and if something was too hard to state in a simple sentence, I didn't bother to say or write it. In other words, I had serious trouble with my Sentence Sense Maker System, which I only found out about when I found your catalog in a trash can near the bus stop. I got some new language parts, and I am quickly becoming a true sentence sense maker. I am a new person. Thank you, <u>Language Parts Catalog.</u> Even my parents are pleased because they don't have to keep repeating instructions to me all the time. Thank you again.

Your Better Listener,
Gretchen

Gretche
21A Wes
Northbo

SECTION 4
The Discourse Developer System

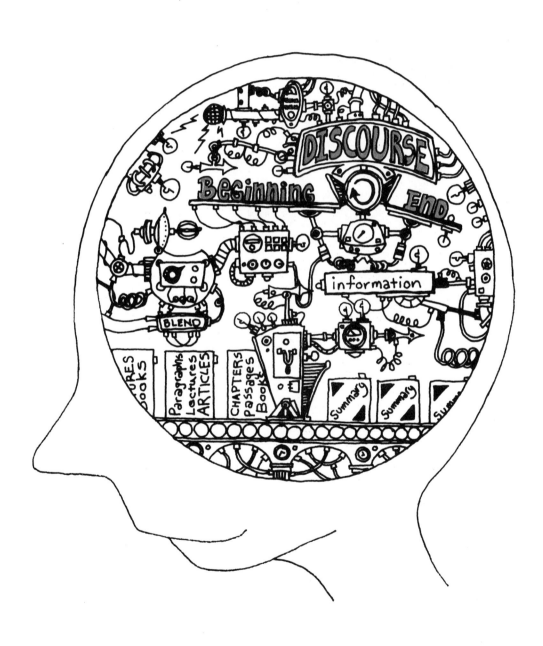

THE DISCOURSE DEVELOPER SYSTEM

Discourse is language that comes in large quantities. It is language that goes beyond single sentences. Discourse is paragraphs, passages, lectures, chapters, articles, and whole books. It can tell a story (a **narrative discourse**) or it can explain some ideas or facts (an **expository discourse**). Discourse is long and takes time to understand. That's why we need our Discourse Developer System, which listens or reads long enough to get all the meaning.

Discourse has some unique characteristics and roles to play. Some of these are listed below:

✓Discourse lets you find out about large amounts of information, or it can be used to explain very complicated ideas.

✓Discourse has to be pretty well organized in order to be understood. Ideas should be presented in the best order. When someone's telling a joke, the punch line needs to arrive at the end, not at the beginning or in the middle. Discourse is a big challenge. The quality of your discourse may show how organized (or disorganized) your mind is!

✓Discourse requires your memory to work closely with your language ability. It is so long that you need to remember the beginning while you're trying to understand the final parts of the message. For example, to appreciate a good story you need to remember how it began and combine that with how it ended. That takes a lot of language memory!

✓Discourse contains all the other parts of language. It is a mixture of language sounds (phonemes), words (semantics), and sentences (syntax). If you are having some problems with one or more of those other parts of language, it can mess up your discourse.

Discourse Developer Parts

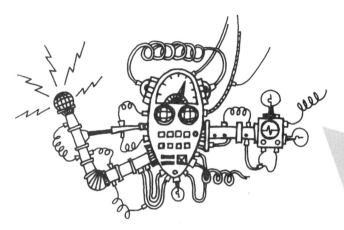

THE READING AND LISTENING RECORDER

Do you ever forget what you're reading while you're reading it? Do you ever lose track of what a teacher is saying? Have you ever forgotten how a joke starts, even though you can remember the punch line? These problems happen to everybody at times, but if they are giving you a lot of trouble, then you can't live without the Reading and Listening Recorder. It helps you store in your mind the early parts of discourse while you're listening to or reading the later parts of it. This is crucial for understanding language that comes in large chunks, such as a chapter in a book.

THE SENTENCE MEANING COMBINER

In discourse a certain sentence often helps you understand the sentence that went before it or after it. For example, "Jake loves pizza with pepperoni. Maria does, too." If you failed to get the first sentence, the second one is useless. Here's another example: "Sara is having a great time. She loves to go fishing." After the first sentence, you have no understanding of why or how Sara is having fun. It takes the second sentence to explain the first one. The Sentence Meaning Combiner helps you combine the

meanings of two or more sentences to form a complete idea in your mind. If you can't keep track of the meaning in two related sentences, you should order the Sentence Meaning Combiner.

THE DISCOURSE SEQUENCER

The all-new Discourse Sequencer helps you get things in the right order when you are listening to or reading instructions, stories, or explanations. If you often have trouble remembering which part of a story happened before another part, or if other kinds of sequences are hard for you, consider ordering this part.

NOTES

_____
_____
_____
_____
_____
_____
_____

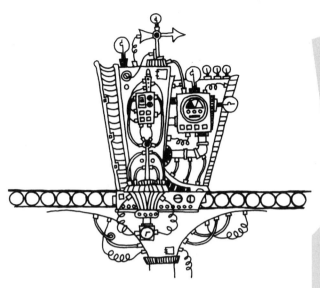

THE PARAPHRASER-SUMMARIZER

This part is key. It lets you listen to or read long (maybe even long-winded) discourse and shorten what was said. The Paraphraser-Summarizer helps you decide what is really important and then makes it easy to condense or abbreviate all the material into a shorter form you can talk or write about. Do you have trouble taking notes when you read or listen? If so, the Paraphraser-Summarizer is just what you need.

THE WRITTEN LANGUAGE BLENDER

To write well you have to combine good language with excellent ideas, accurate spelling, correct punctuation and capitalization, readable handwriting (or good keyboarding), and clear organization. That can be a lot of work. A problem with any of these parts of writing can give you serious trouble with writing and make you feel writing is nothing but trouble! The Written Language Blender helps you combine all the things you need to use excellent language to express super ideas neatly with accurate spelling, punctuation, capitalization, and organization. What more could you ask for? If this kind of blending is tough for you, order this part and become a written language superstar.

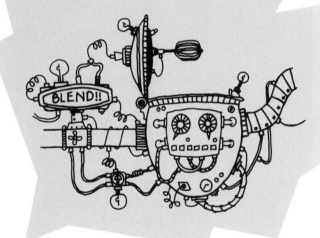

Dear <u>Language Parts Catalog</u>:

Thank you. Thank you. Thank you. I really lucked out when I got your catalog from my friend whose cousin got it from her friend's sister's history teacher's son. Anyway, before I read your catalog, I couldn't figure out why I was getting totally bored and tired during classes when I had to listen to a teacher explain something long and complicated. Also, I had no idea why I seemed to keep losing my concentration and getting completely confused whenever I had to read a chapter in a textbook, even though I am truly super with words and sentences. But after looking through your magnificent, world-famous <u>Language Parts Catalog</u>, I realized that I had some big problems with discourse. It wasn't that I was dumb. It wasn't that I had an attention problem. It wasn't because I didn't care about schoolwork. No way, I was tuning out and spacing out because I was having problems understanding discourse. Somehow my mind couldn't handle language when it came in big portions. I would keep forgetting parts of what I was reading or listening to. Then I would get very mixed-up about what it all meant. Because I didn't understand, I got really bored. Because I was so bored I kept thinking about other things or daydreaming or actually almost falling asleep in class. After all, why stay awake and pay attention to something when you're not understanding or remembering much of it? Now that I have received your Reading and Listening Recorder, my mind is able to hold on to and figure out larger amounts of language input. Also, I am listening harder, taking notes while I listen, and underlining important points while I read. It may be hard to believe, but I can even stay awake in class. You know what? I am now doing super work in school. All of my friends wish that they could understand large chunks of language as well as I do. I have even made new friends, who like the way I am so excellent at understanding language in large quantities. I am enclosing a list of my friends and their addresses. Please send them the <u>Language Parts Catalog</u> before they fall too far behind in school and in their lives. Again, thank you. Thank you. Thank you.

Your friend and fan,
Sofia

Sofia Mala
5886 Kearn
New York

The Language Transmission System

THE LANGUAGE TRANSMISSION SYSTEM

Up until now in this language catalog, we have been featuring mainly parts that can strengthen how well you *understand* different ideas that enter your mind through language (sounds, words, sentences, and discourse). Although we have mentioned speaking and writing as part of some of our parts, we will now fully describe other very crucial ideas and parts having to do with your language *output*, that is, speaking and writing. These abilities rely very much on your mind's Language Transmission System (which is sometimes called your **expressive language**).

Your Language Transmission System has a large number of major jobs to perform, some of which are summarized below:

✓It helps you show others your ideas, feelings, opinions, questions, and knowledge.

✓It helps you organize your thinking. By saying something well, you can understand it better yourself.

✓It helps you remember important things. Your memory may store things better when you put them into words.

✓It helps you make and keep friends. You may need social language (the language kids use when talking with their friends) to be accepted by other kids. We will discuss this in more detail in Section 6 of this catalog.

✓It helps you write down your ideas. Written language depends a lot upon oral language, which is the language you speak. When someone is not a good writer, it may be because he or she isn't much of a speaker!

✓It helps you get your feelings out. If you are very angry or worried or excited it is usually better not to keep all your feelings locked up inside you. Language is a great way to let out at least some of your inner feelings. It may help you feel better to say or write what's on your mind.

✓It can help you control your behavior. It is always good to talk things through, sometimes just to yourself, before behaving a certain way. That may help you realize that what you're about to do could get you into trouble or wreck your relationship with another person. This is called **verbal mediation**. There are some kids who get into trouble partly because they don't use language to help them slow down and control how they act. For example, imagine that you were a basketball player and the referee made a decision you didn't like. You could start arguing or yelling at him. But if you use verbal mediation instead, it would be like a voice inside your mind saying, "I'd better calm down and just walk away. If I argue, I might get thrown out of the game, and my team needs me badly. I won't give the ref a hard time."

✓It helps you plan things better. If you talk about something you are going to do, you may end up doing it better and in a more organized way.

THE THOUGHT ARRANGER

This super part helps you organize your ideas better when you speak or write. You will be able to tell good stories, putting the events in the best order. Your explanations of things will make more sense because you will say your ideas in the best possible order. You will be good at teaching people and giving others instructions that are easy to follow. If any of these tasks are difficult for you, think about ordering this part.

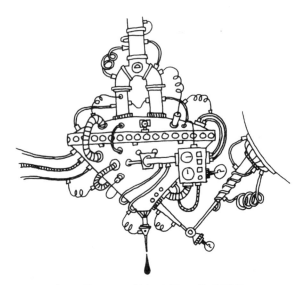

THE FLUENCY LUBRICATOR

Does your speech sometimes sound hesitant, too slow, and just plain too rough? People who talk like that are said to be **dysfluent.** Their spoken language lacks smoothness. Dysfluent people sound as if they are working too hard to get their ideas into words. In other words, they speak as if their language output needs a grease job, so that their words flow smoothly and easily. Does this describe you? Then you may need the Fluency Lubricator.

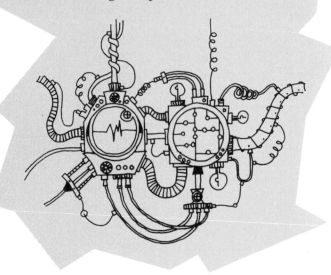

THE SPEECH CLARIFIER

This part is most useful for people whose speech is sometimes hard for others to understand. Do you have trouble pronouncing certain words? Do you have an accent that can make it tough for others to figure out what you mean? Do you sometimes talk too fast and unclearly? If you answered "Yes" to any of these questions, then you need the Speech Clarifier, a remarkable part that helps your tongue, lip, and cheek muscles cooperate better to produce language sounds more clearly.

THE STALL UNINSTALLER

Some people keep using stall words or sounds, such as *like, uh, umm, let me see,* or *you know what I mean.* These are tricks that give a person more time to think of the words or sentences she or he needs to use. But they sound pretty bad when they are used too often. They can make you sound as if you don't know what you're talking about or don't have anything important to say. This exciting new part helps you cut back on those unattractive stall words. Is "like" the most-used word in your vocabulary? What about "you know"? Don't stall any longer—order the Stall Uninstaller.

Hi, Language Catalog:

I have like just gotten my Stall Uninstaller part? Like this is something I've like really needed, like for years I've needed this? Up till now I've had to keep like stalling like when I talk to get the time to like find like the words I need? Like now I won't need to just like say words like "like" that I don't even like because all those "likes" sound alike when I like talk to people I like, you know what I mean? Once I like get rid of the "likes" I really dislike, then I'll work on trying not to make every sentence like sound like a question? I think that's called "upspeak"? My mom will be so happy? Like, thanks so much. Now I like know that I'm like likely to sound really cool—unlike the way I like talk now?

Likewise I'm sure,
Lydia??

Lydia E
8 Cabir
St. Paul,

THE LANGUAGE ELABORATOR

Verbal elaborating means stretching and connecting ideas by talking or writing about them. Some kids almost never elaborate on anything. They answer questions by saying "yeah," or "cool," or "I guess." If a non-elaborator's mom asked him, "What did you do in school today?", he might say, "Stuff." A good elaborator might say something like, "Well, in science we learned about frogs and toads, and tomorrow Mr. Alvarez is going to bring in a real live frog for us to look at." Good elaborators go into detail. Kids who don't elaborate may not even talk in complete sentences very often. Sometimes these students have a lot of trouble doing schoolwork. They hate to get called on in class because it is hard for them to elaborate on their ideas. Also, students who don't elaborate on what they are studying have trouble remembering the material later on tests. They might remember that the American Revolution began in 1776, but to do well on a test, they'll probably need to know a lot more than that, such as the reasons the war started. One of the best ways to retain information is to elaborate on it. So, if you are a genuine non-elaborator, if this sounds like you, do not hesitate. Start using the wonderful Language Elaborator as soon as possible.

NOTES

_____

_____

_____

_____

_____

_____

_____

_____

HIGH-FREQUENCY AND LOW-FREQUENCY WORDS

Note: Some words are very common and get used all the time in everyday speech. They are called **high-frequency vocabulary**. Words like *home, go, happy, there,* and *hungry* are all part of a high-frequency vocabulary, the words everyone uses often. But words like *henceforth, expeditiously,* and *clandestine* are low-frequency words, which are not used so often. A good speaker mixes high-frequency words with some low-frequency words when she or he speaks. A person with language transmission weaknesses may only use high-frequency words, never (or hardly ever) using tough or unusual words. That's usually okay when you're with your friends. They don't mind if you use ordinary words. Your best friend is unlikely to say, "Please stop speaking with all those high-frequency words." But good schoolwork often demands that you use low-frequency words to interpret and explain complicated ideas or facts. So keep adding low-frequency words to your talking (and writing) in school. You'll even start using many of them outside of school. Then you'll be able to talk about more complicated ideas than you ever could before.

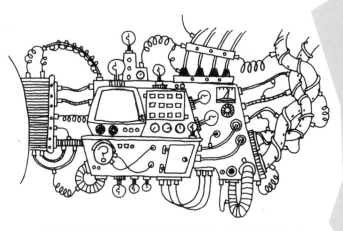

THE CREATIVE THOUGHT GENERATOR

Language is a great way to be original, to exercise your imagination and think up new ideas. Using language you can create stories, jokes, or poems; think up new inventions; and form ideas no one else has formed. No longer will you need to imitate and overuse the same old ideas. Our Creative Thought Generator will help you become your own unique new-idea person. If you like the sound of that, order this part and start creating!

NOTES

THE MISSING WORD AND NAME LOCATOR

Do you ever have trouble remembering the right word or name for something? Is it on the tip of your tongue, but you just can't think of it? Do you have trouble participating in class discussions because you can never find the exact words you need fast enough? If this is happening too often, if it is making it hard for you to keep up with talk in class, consider investing in the remarkable new Missing Word and Name Locator. You, too, can be quick on the draw when it comes to words you really know but that you can't think of the second you need them.

Dear Language Catalog Company,

I never used to say anything, mostly "yes," "no," "stuff," and, of course, "thing." Then my older brother told me that my Discourse Developer System wasn't developing. My Language Transmission System wasn't transmitting too well, either. So I ordered your famous catalog and started working on my problem. Now I like to elaborate, so that my friends, parents, other relatives, neighbors, the mail carrier, the salespeople at the mall, and my teachers and the school principal will be able to hear everything I have on my mind. That way there will be no misunderstandings, and I will have a chance to communicate my ideas at length, even when I have to use complex sentences and long explanations to accomplish this important effort in school, at home, in the neighborhood, and wherever my path in life may carry me over the coming years of my education and in other parts of my existence. Thank you so much for helping me learn to elaborate, although it is possible that I am now over-elaborating. Please send me your Discourse Abbreviator if you have one, so that I do not overdo the large chunks of language output that I have learned to produce as a result of ordering your fine language parts. Oops, I'm running out of paper.

Yours sincerely,

Oscar

Oscar W
63 Rutl
Oshkosh

SECTION 6
The Language Socializer System

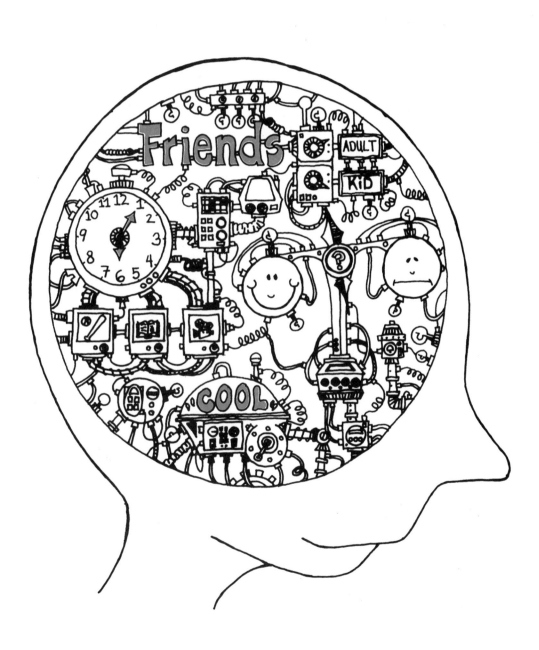

THE LANGUAGE SOCIALIZER SYSTEM

Believe it or not, language can do a lot to help a person make and keep friends and have a good reputation. The way you talk can affect how other kids (and adults) think of you. Your language ability can also help you figure out what other kids really mean when they say something to you, which can help you decide how to treat them or talk to them. The part of language that affects friendship and popularity we will call **social language**. Language experts call this **verbal pragmatics**. Whatever you call it, your social language ability is very important all your life. By the way, it is possible to be very strong with other parts of language and have trouble with social language. And there are some kids who are great with social language but have trouble with **literate language**, the language needed to do well in school subjects.

Of course, not everybody wants to be popular. Many kids enjoy spending time by themselves and doing their own things without always trying to please others in their age group. It is important to keep your social life in balance. Otherwise, you might waste all of your time working too hard to sound cool, win friends, and be very popular. Then schoolwork and other important parts of your life can suffer badly. So, your social language abilities should work well for you when you need them to. But don't feel you have to use them all the time. Remember to be yourself.

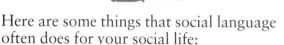

Here are some things that social language often does for your social life:

✓It helps you sound "cool" when you want to.

✓It helps you win arguments or have discussions without hurting other people's feelings.

✓It helps you have some control over other people without having to avoid them completely or act tough with them.

✓It helps you let people know how you feel about them in general or about something they have said or done.

Language Socializer Parts

THE CODE SWITCHER

You shouldn't talk the same exact way to everyone you meet. Kids need to switch language codes, depending upon whom they are with. You don't speak the same way to a police officer, your mom, your best friend, your two-year-old sister, and your new teacher. The tone of your voice, the words you pick, the length of your sentences, and many other adjustments get made when you're with different kinds of people. Some kids sound *too* smart when they talk. They may sound too much like a grown-up. Their parents may really like the way they talk, but other kids don't. They may even be jealous. But a kid who speaks like that may have to do it all the time. He can't switch to a kid code when he's with other kids. The Code Switcher helps you decide how to fit your language to the listener. If you've been having trouble with code switching, consider ordering this part so you can start adjusting your language.

THE MOOD PROCESSOR

This socializer part does two things: it helps you *talk* in a way that shows your true feelings, and it helps you *listen* in a way that lets you understand other people's true feelings. The Mood Processor prevents you from sounding angry when you're not really angry or sounding sad when you're feeling okay or sounding too much as if you're serious when you're only kidding. The Mood Processor stops people from misunderstanding your feelings. You can also use it to decide how someone else is feeling. That way you won't talk about something silly if a person looks sad or say something sad when everyone is telling jokes and having fun. Do you find yourself saying the wrong thing when you don't notice someone else's mood? Do people read your moods wrong? Then you may need the Mood Processor.

THE MOOD MATCHER

You can use your Mood Processor to figure out other people's current moods. Are they happy or sad or angry? Then use your Mood Matcher to help you fit the mood of your words and sentences to the mood of other people you are with. If a bunch of kids are laughing and having fun, that is not the moment to move in and tell them about something very sad. If, on the other hand, some students are discussing a serious topic, something about which they are extremely concerned or angry, that may not be the time to tell a joke or say something very silly. It is often necessary to adjust the tone of your voice, the words you choose, and what you talk about to fit the present feelings of other people. If you're having trouble matching moods, think about ordering this terrific part.

THE HUMOR REGULATOR

Humor is an important way for people to enjoy being together, and language is a major part of humor. People really like people who know how to use humor well. On the other hand, if you tell a joke and you are the only person laughing at it (and don't even realize no one else is laughing), that can be a definite social problem for you. The Humor Regulator lets you use language to pick just the right kind of humor for the people you are with. It also tells you whether people think you're being funny or not, so you don't look foolish in public. In other words, if listeners don't think you're funny (even though you're trying to be funny), you should probably try out some other kind of humor or find people who think you're funny just the way you are. If you want humor skills that are suitable for all occasions, however, consider ordering the Humor Regulator.

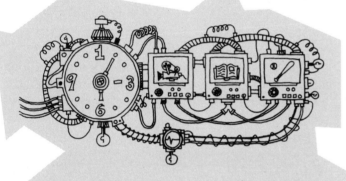

THE TOPIC SELECTOR AND TIMER

This valuable part helps you decide what to talk about and how long to talk about it. Some people really turn off others by always talking about inappropriate topics. Or they might talk about things for too long and everyone gets bored, angry, or annoyed. The Topic Selector and Timer helps you choose the right topic for the right audience at the right time, and it tells you when to stop and switch to a new subject. If people start yawning when you talk, or suddenly remember something else they have to do, you might need the Topic Selector and Timer.

THE CONFLICT SOLVER

Language is a great tool for solving problems. Friends always have times when they're not getting along as well or when they have real disagreements about something. That's when good social language can come to the rescue! By talking out your problems, you and your friend can work everything out without any physical violence and without having to end a good friendship. The Conflict Solver finds you the language you need to solve problems through honest discussion. If you have trouble talking over disagreements with people without having everybody get extremely upset, you may need this part.

THE LANGUAGE LINGO LEARNER

Kids like to have their own language. They enjoy using some slang words that most adults never say. Sometimes these words come from TV shows or music lyrics, and sometimes they seem to come from nowhere and spread rapidly to students everywhere. The words change over time. They have included terms like *phat, chill out, awesome, geek, dude,* and *neat-o.* How good are you at speaking the language (the lingo) of other kids? Some students are truly amazing in their use of the language of their friends, while others don't sound right when they try to use the lingo that's in style. What about

you? If you have trouble talking like other kids, you definitely need the updated update of the Language Lingo Learner.

THE SOCIAL LANGUAGE INTERPRETER

This terrific part helps you decide what people really and truly mean when they say something. This is necessary because the actual words people use do not always show what they mean to say. If someone at lunch says, "Can you pass the mustard?" you are not supposed to just sit there and say, "Yes." You should pass the mustard. Although it may have sounded like it, that person was not trying to find out if you have the ability to pass mustard; she just wanted some mustard. The Social Language Interpreter helps you get underneath the basic words people use to find out their true desires. If you've been having a tough time figuring out what people really want, order this part today.

Dear Friendly Language Catalog,

I used to have no friends at all. Throughout the day, everyone would say to me, "Sorry, this seat is saved." I couldn't figure out what I was doing wrong, but other kids seemed to avoid me. At home when the telephone rang, it was always for my sister, never for me. I used to play alone all the time, but I wished I had friends and could be popular. Then one day your catalog arrived in the mail. I threw it away, but my dog took it out of the trash can and completely tore up the sections on language sounds, word meaning, sentences, and discourse. I don't have trouble with those parts of language. The dog left the social section alone. I quickly read that section of the catalog. I was totally shocked. Yes, that was me.

I immediately thanked my dog for leaving me that part of the <u>Language Parts Catalog.</u> How come I never before realized that it was hard for me to talk right with other kids? I had problems using slang the right way. No one ever laughed at my jokes or could tell when I was kidding or serious. I always seemed to talk about the wrong things and boasted much too much. I was never told how important language is for getting along with others. Now I know. I saved up my money and ordered those social language parts. They were worth it. I have been working on social language, and now the telephone rings for me. I have good friends, and we spend a lot of time talking, having great discussions. I don't seem to bug anyone anymore with the way I talk. Thank you, <u>Language Parts Catalog,</u> for helping me get along with others. By the way, do you have a <u>Language Parts Catalog</u> for dogs? Mine never follows directions.

Your Friendly Friend,
Paul

Paul Ch
31 Smith
Atlanta,

SOME FINAL DISCOURSE

Now that you have had a chance to find out about all the vital roles of language in school and in life, take the time to think about yourself and your own language abilities. No one is perfect in all aspects of language. Think carefully about the parts of your different language systems. If you made some notes along the way, you might want to take another look at those now. Then complete the enclosed order form to decide which language parts you need, so that language can become a really good partner, a fantastic help to you as you go through life in school and beyond.

ATTENTION: Please fill out your order form right away.

Now that you know about all the exciting language parts that are available, you should place your order promptly. Start working to improve your language abilities.

THE *LANGUAGE PARTS CATALOG* ORDER FORM

Use these pages to decide what new parts you will need to improve *your* language ability.

Directions: After reading the catalog, please fill out the form completely. You can look back in the catalog if you get confused about any of the parts on the order form.

SECTION I — PARTS FOR THE LANGUAGE SOUND PROCESSING SYSTEM

Language Part and What You Can Do with It	Need a Whole Lot	Need	Need a Little	Already Good at This
The Rapid Sound Sensor: Process the sounds in language quickly and accurately	❏	❏	❏	❏
The Language Sound Transmitter: Pronounce language sounds (and words) quickly and easily	❏	❏	❏	❏
The Rhymer: Tell what words sound a lot like other words; write poetry and song lyrics	❏	❏	❏	❏
The Sound-to-Symbol Attacher: Remember what sounds go with what letters (for reading and spelling)	❏	❏	❏	❏
The Sound Splitter: Break a word down into the sounds it is made of	❏	❏	❏	❏
The Sound Blender: Build words out of their sounds, help reading and spelling	❏	❏	❏	❏
The Foreign Sound Processor: Learn the sounds in a new language	❏	❏	❏	❏
The Sound Inflector: Emphasize certain sounds in words to pronounce the words correctly	❏	❏	❏	❏
The Language Sound Finder: Remember words and names by knowing the sound they start with or contain	❏	❏	❏	❏
The Total Language Sound Processor: Perform all the above tasks using one part that improves your whole system	❏	❏	❏	❏

SECTION 2 – PARTS FOR THE WORD MEANING SYSTEM

Language Part and What You Can Do with It	Need a Whole Lot	Need	Need Little	Already Good at This
The Word Builder: Create real whole words by knowing the meanings of word parts	❑	❑	❑	❑
The Semantic Network Builder: Connect all the words you know on a big map in your mind	❑	❑	❑	❑
The Vocabulary Memorizer: Learn the meanings of new words and be able to use the words well	❑	❑	❑	❑
The Word Meaning Stretcher: Know all the different meanings and uses of the words you know	❑	❑	❑	❑
The Technical Word Learner: Learn the hard words that are used mainly in school (as in science vocabulary)	❑	❑	❑	❑
The Abstract Word Learner: Learn words that are hard to picture in your mind	❑	❑	❑	❑
The Written Word Decoder: Be able to read totally new words	❑	❑	❑	❑
The Word Classifier: Fully understand parts of speech and how to use them	❑	❑	❑	❑

SECTION 3 – PARTS FOR THE SENTENCE SENSE MAKER SYSTEM

Language Part and What You Can Do with It	Need a Whole Lot	Need	Need Little	Already Good at This
The Grammar Applicator and Checker: Speak absolutely correct English, using good grammar	❑	❑	❑	❑
The Sentence Writer: Put your thoughts into good sentences when you write	❑	❑	❑	❑
The Speedy Sentence Synthesizer: Put your thoughts into good sentences when speaking	❑	❑	❑	❑
The Speedy Sentence Translator: Understand other people's sentences quickly and accurately	❑	❑	❑	❑
The Sentence Reader: Find the most meaning in sentences that you read	❑	❑	❑	❑

The Figurative Figure-er: Really know what others mean when they don't actually say what they mean	❏	❏	❏	❏
The Conjunctionizer: Make very impressive complex sentences with words like *although* and *unless*	❏	❏	❏	❏

SECTION 4 – PARTS FOR THE DISCOURSE DEVELOPER SYSTEM

Language Part and What You Can Do with It	Need a Whole Lot	Need	Need a Little	Already Good at This
The Reading and Listening Recorder: Remember and understand what you are reading or hearing	❏	❏	❏	❏
The Sentence Meaning Combiner: Add the meanings of more than one sentence to get a whole message	❏	❏	❏	❏
The Discourse Sequencer: Keep ideas in the right order in your mind while listening or reading	❏	❏	❏	❏
The Paraphraser-Summarizer: Make language shorter without losing what's important in it	❏	❏	❏	❏
The Written Language Blender: Combine good language with spelling, punctuation, and other parts of writing	❏	❏	❏	❏

SECTION 5 – PARTS FOR THE LANGUAGE TRANSMISSION SYSTEM

Language Part and What You Can Do with It	Need a Whole Lot	Need	Need a Little	Already Good at This
The Thought Arranger: Organize your ideas the best way as you put them into language	❏	❏	❏	❏
The Speech Clarifier: Pronounce words better and talk in a way others can understand easily	❏	❏	❏	❏
The Fluency Lubricator: Talk easily and quickly enough, so you can keep up with others and sound interesting	❏	❏	❏	❏
The Stall Uninstaller: Stop using different meaningless delay sounds or words while you are speaking	❏	❏	❏	❏
The Language Elaborator: Use language to think through and express ideas in enough detail	❏	❏	❏	❏
The Creative Thought Generator: Come up with interesting and original ideas with language	❏	❏	❏	❏

| The Missing Word and Name Locator: Find words that are on the tip of your tongue whenever you need them | ❏ | ❏ | ❏ | ❏ |

SECTION 6 — PARTS FOR THE LANGUAGE SOCIALIZER SYSTEM

Language Part and What You Can Do with It	Need a Whole Lot	Need	Need a Little	Already Good at This
The Code Switcher: Know how to talk differently to different people you are with	❏	❏	❏	❏
The Mood Processor: Use language to understand other people's feelings and let them know yours	❏	❏	❏	❏
The Mood Matcher: Speak in a way that fits the mood other people are in	❏	❏	❏	❏
The Topic Selector and Timer: Pick the right topic to speak about and know just how long to continue	❏	❏	❏	❏
The Humor Regulator: Appreciate other people's humor and be good at using your humor	❏	❏	❏	❏
The Conflict Solver: Use language to fix disagreements you have	❏	❏	❏	❏
The Language Lingo Learner: Speak the way other kids do	❏	❏	❏	❏
The Social Language Interpreter: Figure out what people expect from you and want you to know when they speak	❏	❏	❏	❏

Now that you have completed your order form, and before you get further behind in your language abilities, there are several things you can do with the form:

1. Call in your order to (_____) _____-_____.
   (Please fill in your home phone number.)

2. Put a copy in a time capsule and read it in 50 years.

3. Give a copy to your teacher and a copy to your parents.

4. Keep it, review it, and think of ways you can improve your own language abilities now that you know what you need to improve (see instructions on page 59).

5. All of the above.

What to Do While Waiting for
Your Language Part(s) to Arrive

When you order a part, it means that you have made up your mind that you want to improve your language abilities. Unfortunately, we have been so flooded with orders that our parts department can take months to ship out the parts. In the meantime, you can read some of the instructions that will come with your part. They will tell you what you can do to build up your language abilities.

LANGUAGE PARTS INSTRUCTIONS

For Language Sound Processing Parts

✓Try to think of a word and find as many real words as you can that rhyme with it. Compete with your friends.

✓Practice playing Pig Latin. This is a game that gives your mind practice working with language sounds. To play the game, you take a word and move its first sound to the end of the word and then add the sound "ay." For example, the word *goose* becomes *oosegay* and the word *think* becomes *inkthay*. Practice making these word changes, and see if you can talk in full sentences in Pig Latin. By the way, this language can be excellent when you don't want your little brother or sister to know what you are saying to your friends over the telephone.

✓Look at some long, complicated words, separate them into their individual sounds, and then blend them all together. You may want to start with short words until you get pretty good at this activity.

✓Try moving around certain sounds in a word and then trying to pronounce the new word.

✓There are 44 language sounds in English. List and pronounce as many of these as you can. Then practice saying them as fast as you can.

✓Put individual language sounds on cards. Then try this game (called Phoneme Poker): Deal each person five cards. Nobody should let anyone else see their cards. Each person sees how many real words he can make from his five cards in two minutes. The words should be written down. Each person can then put back two cards and take two more if he wants. Then he tries to make some new words with the new sounds. The winner of each round is the person who can make the most words from his language sound cards. You can think up your own scoring system for this game.

✓You and a friend can each make up a list of 10 to 20 nonsense words that have at least four real language sounds in them. Make sure these are words that can be pronounced in English. Then see how quickly your friend can read them accurately. Then you should try reading his or her list.

For Word Meaning Parts

✓Do crossword puzzles, play Scrabble and Boggle, and try playing other word games.

✓Create some semantic maps, like the one for *mule* shown on the next page. Do this with some difficult words. Show the different things you might think of when you see or hear a particular word.

SEMANTIC MAP OF THE WORD *MULE*

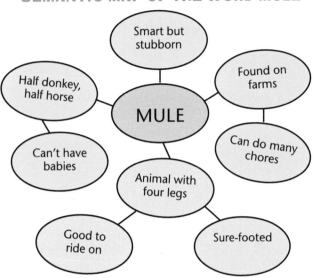

✓Make a real effort to use new words soon after you first learn them. The best way to understand and remember new vocabulary is to use it. Don't keep using the same old words all the time. For one thing, that's boring. For another, people who just use common words (high-frequency vocabulary) all the time can sound pretty dull. They usually don't make a very good impression.

✓Know which subjects in school have a lot of new vocabulary, especially technical words. For these subjects you should keep a personal dictionary of the words that you seem to have trouble remembering. The dictionary can be on paper or in a computer.

For Sentence Sense Maker Parts

✓Whenever possible, concentrate on speaking in complete sentences instead of speaking a lot in single words or very short phrases.

✓Try to pay attention when you're learning about grammar and how it works. Some kids find this boring, but it really helps you understand and use sentences more accurately.

✓Here's a sentence-building game you can play: Give someone three words and see how long it takes her to make a complete sentence (in good English) using the words you gave her. Then it's her turn to challenge you with three words. Hint: Try to include words that force the person to make up a complex sentence (conjunctions like *unless*, *although*, and *until*).

✓When you write, try to use more than one kind of sentence in each paragraph. Don't just write in simple sentences; mix them up, use some complex and compound ones. You should try to do that when you talk, too. Here are some examples. The first one just uses boring simple sentences:

> *Mark went home. He had supper. He studied. He called Jaime. Then he went to bed.*

Here's how this can sound better when you mix the kinds of sentences that are used:

> *Mark went home as soon as school was over [a complex sentence]. He ate his supper and studied for a test [a compound sentence]. Before going to bed, he talked to Jaime on the telephone for a few minutes [another complex sentence]. Then he fell asleep [a simple sentence].*

Mixing up your sentences like this makes your language sound better, and it's a lot more interesting to listen to.

For Discourse Developer Parts

✓Learn how to listen carefully when someone important is speaking about something important. Often you can tell when a teacher is saying something key because that idea or fact gets emphasized by the teacher's tone of voice or it gets repeated one or more times.

✓Always read textbooks or complicated stories with some way to record ideas as you go along. That includes underlining key points (if you own the book or article), dictating critical ideas into a pocket tape recorder, or making little notes on Post-its that you have attached to each page before reading.

✓Practice summarizing to yourself (or on paper or into a tape recorder) after you listen to or read discourse. You can summarize individual sentences after you hear them (as long as you don't miss out on the speaker's next sentences) or do an entire paragraph's worth of summarizing.

✓Learn to take good notes. That also helps you concentrate while you're listening to long explanations or instructions.

✓Form visual images in your mind while listening or reading. Making pictures in your mind improves your understanding and memory of what you are listening to.

✓Try to predict what's coming next while reading or listening. This helps your attention while improving your understanding.

✓Reading is probably the best way to get excellent with discourse. Try to read books and articles about subjects that really interest you. Become an expert by reading a lot of things about one topic or area. Having a lot of knowledge about something actually improves your reading comprehension and your language abilities. Subscribe to a magazine about a subject that interests you and read it thoroughly whenever it comes out. Newspapers are great for your language development too, even the sports pages. Most television shows, on the other hand, don't improve anyone's language abilities. That's because language on television is usually very simple. Also, because there are pictures, most people don't listen to the language very carefully, so television doesn't require much language ability. Nor does it encourage you to practice using language. Finally, television is usually very passive. That means you don't have to think very

hard, and you don't have to use your Language Transmission System at all while sitting on a couch watching TV. Too much television can actually prevent you from getting good with language!

For Language Transmission Parts

✓Elaborate whenever you can. Don't just keep giving very short answers (like *yeah, cool,* and *I guess*). Extend your ideas, add details. When you elaborate, your language skills improve. Elaboration also helps you remember and understand.

✓Make oral presentations when you can. They should be on topics that interest you and that you know a lot about. That way you can concentrate on your language instead of worrying about knowing your topic.

✓Do some teaching. Explain to your friend how to do something or practice teaching your younger brother or sister or cousin. Teaching is one of the best ways to learn, and it strengthens your language transmitter at the same time.

✓Whenever you do a difficult math problem or complete a project in school, try explaining to someone else how you did it. Explaining things you've done is a great way to develop better language output. Use complete sentences and try to organize your explanation, so that you say things clearly and in the best possible order.

✓Describe your experiences. Organizing a narrative is a very good way to improve language. (Narrative is language output that describes events that happened in a particular order.)

✓ Try to keep a journal or diary. Recording things that happen to you each day is a great way to get good at building your own discourse. By the way, don't worry about spelling and grammar at first—concentrate on using language. Later you can work on the technical stuff.

✓Practice summarizing out loud or on paper things you've read, TV shows you've watched, or movies you've seen. Ask yourself about the most important parts of what you've seen or heard. Then arrange these ideas in the best, most organized order in your mind.

For Language Socializer Parts

✓Pay attention to students whom you think talk well socially. Try to figure out how they use certain words and sentences that make them sound right with other kids.

✓Watch carefully to see how others are reacting when you speak. If they ignore you, don't laugh at funny things you say, or laugh at serious things you say, there may be something wrong with the way you are talking.

✓Practice using "in" or "cool" words in sentences, both with other kids and when you're just thinking to yourself.

✓Don't use language to try to sound super smart or too superior when you are with other kids. Make sure you're not boasting all the time. Kids usually don't like that very much, because they might feel jealous or feel as if you're looking down on them. Use your Language Socializer System to make other kids feel good about themselves, just as you would like it if they said nice things to you. Learn how to praise them. Use language to show them that you admire and respect them. (Of course, don't say things unless you really mean them.)

✓Make sure your feelings are not being misunderstood when you speak. If people think you sound angry when you don't mean to, that's a problem. You may need to practice matching up the way you speak with how you feel.

✓Keep in mind that you should not talk exactly the same way to everyone. Think about the people you see every day and how it is important to talk a little differently to your teacher, your mom, your friend, a new kid in class, an adult you just met, and your brother or sister. Be yourself, but try to remember that this kind of code switching is an important ability.

A FEW CONCLUDING WORDS (AND SENTENCES AND DISCOURSE)

Now that you have had a chance to think about language and its many parts and the new parts you may need, you can keep thinking about words, sentences, and other aspects of language while you are using language. You can become a better writer and a more interesting speaker in class. You can be more careful about how you talk to other people, so that they will like and respect you. You can also impress yourself with how much easier it is to think about complicated matters when your language functions are working well. It's just plain true that being excellent with language is one way to become a much more intelligent person. No matter what you want to do when you get older, good language ability can help you do it better. So go for it! Never stop working on your ability to understand, create, and communicate thoughts through language.